Alaska
on my mind

More than just a bump on a log, this brown bear loafs among the driftwood KENNAN WARD

" *People hear the word 'Alaska,' and it's magic all over the world.*
It just seems to get everybody's imagination stirred up. "

Joan Daniels
as quoted in *"I'd Swap My Old Skidoo for You"*

FALCON®

Ice, snow, and sheer cliffs define the rugged, wild beauty of the Alaska Range ART WOLFE

3

Bald eagle on approach in the
Tongass National Forest JOHN HYDE

Lush vegetation blankets the floor of the coastal rain forest on Admiralty Island, along Alaska's Inside Passage ROBIN BRANDT

Cooper Creek plunges through slippery stepping stones of the Chugach Mountains JAMES RANDKLEV

In Denali National Park, cottongrass mimics the August whiteness of Mt. McKinley CARR CLIFTON

On Polychrome Mountain in Denali National Park, Dall sheep rams rest with eyes alert for their main predator, the wolf LARRY ULRICH

" The Alaskan sheep does not resemble those of Montana and other sheep countries. It is more delicate and far more beautiful. There is a deerlike grace in the poise of its head, a fine and sensitive outline to nostril and mouth, a tenderness in the great dark eyes, that is at once startled and appealing; while the wide, graceful sweep of the horns is unrivalled."

Ella Higginson
Alaska: The Great Country

Blueberries and red kinnikinnick berries punctuate the palette of September colors in the tundra foliage of Denali National Park ART WOLFE

> *The Arctic has strange stillness that no other wilderness knows. It has loneliness too—a feeling of isolation and remoteness born of vast spaces, the rolling tundra, and the barren domes of limestone mountains. This is a loneliness that is joyous and exhilarating. All the noises of civilization have been left behind; now the music of the wilderness can be heard.*

William O. Douglas
My Wilderness: The Pacific West

A willow ptarmigan in fall plumage makes tracks
ALISSA CRANDALL

9

Spruce trees stand like spectators gathered loosely on an autumn hillside along the Denali Highway JAMES RANDLKLEV

This grizzly claims his territory along Anan Creek in the Tongass National Forest CLIFF RIEDLINGER

Arctic ground squirrel ROBIN BRANDT

" Then, late in the third day, as they approached a wooded break in the canyon, the bear, who was now only a short distance ahead of them, stopped again. He turned, rose once more to a thick and imposing presence, and looked steadily at the men gathered behind him. . . .It was the assured and measuring look of the undisputed master of things. "

John Haines
The Stars, the Snow, the Fire

11

Rustic buildings reflect in Hammer Slough in Petersburg JEFF GNASS

Getting ready to go somewhere? GARY LACKIE

Sea kayakers assemble in Ketchikan TOM AND PAT LEESON

A shed caribou antler accents the graceful slopes of the Sadlerochit Mountains
in the Arctic National Wildlife Refuge SCOTT T. SMITH

The Sheenjek River drains a wilderness valley in the Brooks Range, Arctic National Wildlife Refuge   CARR CLIFTON

A gray wolf streaks past with a jaw full of ground squirrel   RON SANFORD

66 This is the value of this piece of wilderness—its absolutely untouched character. Not spectacular, no unique or 'strange' features, but just the beautiful, wild country of a beautiful, wild free-running river, with no sign of man or his structures. For this feature alone this Arctic is worth preserving just as it is. 99

Margaret E. Murie
Two In The Far North

Enjoying a backcountry skiing adventure on Admiralty Island, just south of Juneau   JOHN HYDE

❝ *What distinguishes life in Alaska from life in other States? For one thing, the unspoiled wilderness, with all its abundance, beauty, and mystery is always nearby. . . .But perhaps most important, the last frontier is inhabited by the friendliest people. There is neither caste nor class in Alaska. Here are no status seekers.*

Being both Americans and Alaskans is status enough. ❞

Ernest Gruening
from his *"Address to the American Meteorological Society"*

Minus five degrees at Denali National Park makes it a great day for a mountain bike ride   CRAIG BRANDT

South of Anchorage, cliffs in Chugach State Park provide excellent practice for all levels of ice climbers HARRY M. WALKER

A musher and team freight supplies for climbers on Muldrow Glacier in Denali National Park ROLLIE OSTERMICK

66 . . . so long will the dog be hitched to the sled in Alaska; so long will his joyful yelp and his plaintive whine be heard in the land; so long will his warm tongue seek his master's hand . . .and his eloquent eyes speak his utter allegiance.99

Hudson Stuck
Ten Thousand Miles With a Dog Sled

A clear day and a good trail for musher and team enroute to Nome in the Iditarod, "the last great race" JANE GNASS

These sled dogs get a comfy box stuffed with straw while their owner relaxes in the steamy baths of Chena Hot Springs KENNAN WARD

Decorated longhouse and totems in Totem Bight State Park near Ketchikan, part of the efforts to preserve the native heritage of Southeast Alaska TOM TILL

Artisan and her craft in Anaktuvuk Pass LEE FOSTER

Tree and tradition, root and myth, Sitka spruce and the Yaadaas Crest Corner Pole find sanctuary
in the Sitka National Historical Park JEFF GNASS

Often seen along the Inside Passage, the orca is glorious to behold when it pierces the air TOM AND PAT LEESON

The pride of the Pribilofs, this northern fur seal sizes up a possible challenge to its claim of these rocks on St. Paul Island ROBIN BRANDT

A nest on a rocky pinnacle in the Gulf of Alaska is prime real estate for a bald eagle TOM AND PAT LEESON

A collection of floats and "corks" for fishing nets hang in the August sun outside a boathouse in Petersburg JEFF GNASS

" *To a fisherman, every fishing day is like Christmas, every net like presents to be opened. We never know what surprises we might find, only that there'll be something there and that it just might be, this time, the stuff of our dreams.* "

Nancy Lord
Fishcamp

King crab caught off the Aleutian Islands LON E. LAUBER

A rare moment of peace before a hectic summer fishing season in Kodiak Harbor JEFF GNASS

Bone-white clamshells litter the black rock shoreline of West Chichagof Yakobi Wilderness north of Sitka CARR CLIFTON

Starfish at low tide appear to march from the waters of Gambier Bay in the Admiralty Island National Monument CARR CLIFTON

The red-faced cormorant is an uncommon sighting
for bird enthusiasts JOHN HYDE

*" The land and the water are our sources of life.
The water is sacred. The water is like a baptismal
font, and its abundance is the Holy Communion of
our lives. . .The water is our source of life."*

Walter Meganack, Sr.
"When the Water Died" in *Season of Dead Water*

Spare peaks and tenacious vegetation contribute to the beauty of the Brooks Range CARR CLIFTON

Caribou with full racks swim the Kobuk River during fall migration ROLLIE OSTERMICK

Erratic boulders contrast with the shorn look of the Sadlerochit Mountains above the Arctic Circle on the North Slope of the Brooks Range SCOTT T. SMITH

A galaxy of glaucous-winged gulls crowd the air on the Kenai Peninsula HENRY H. HOLDSWORTH

66 Great wilderness has two characteristics: remoteness, and the presence of wild animals in something like pristine variety and numbers. Remoteness cannot be imitated in cheap materials; and wilderness without animals is mere scenery. 99

Lois Crisler
Arctic Wild

The largest, most aggressive grizzly gets the best fishing spot on the McNeil River TOM AND PAT LEESON

Bears of a feather HENRY H. HOLDSWORTH

A vista of rugged peace during fall in the Chilkat River Valley JOHN HYDE

" There is one other asset of the Territory not yet enumerated—imponderable and difficult to appraise, yet one of the chief assets of Alaska, if not the greatest. This is the scenery. There are glaciers, mountains, and fiords elsewhere, but nowhere else on earth is there such abundance and magnificence of mountain, fiord, and glacier scenery. "

Henry Gannett
Harriman Alaska Expedition, 1899

33

A common loon arches in dramatic gesture GARY LACKIE

Snow clings to the peaks year-round, but it is shorts weather backpacking through fall tundra in Denali National Park RICH REID

34

A handful of cloudberries picked on the coastal plain of the
Arctic National Wildlife Refuge SCOTT T. SMITH

Sunny fall days are perfect for playing in the intense colors of alpine tundra in Denali National Park ROLLIE OSTERMICK

Moose cow and calf rub noses in a reassuring greeting R.E. BARBER

Poisonous and alluring, the fly amanita is named for the
belief that a toxin it produces kills flies GARY LACKIE

Black lilly, black beauty ROBIN BRANDT

Lupine find room to grow at the edge of Mendenhall Glacier near Juneau TOM TILL

The subtle green infusion of summer on the slopes near Igloo Mountain in Denali National Park TOM BEAN

One of the numerous fingers of Prince William Sound: Harriman Fiord with Mount Muir in the background GEORGE WUERTHNER

The fixed stare of a hawk owl ART WOLFE

“ No care is so sure as a good wild solitude. The old sages knew its worth & shamans & prophets & Christ even felt the need of solitude. ”

John Muir
as quoted in *Henry Thoreau and John Muir Among the Indians*

A house post flashes a toothy grin inside Chief Shakes Tribal House in Wrangell JOHN HYDE

For the traditional native people, Alaska is not a raw frontier. It's their home. They're not here for some kind of thrill or to prove something. They're here because they've been here for a thousand years in traceable generations or longer. . .It's not a place where you fulfill fantasies. It's a place where you live in measured consonance with the way the world is.

Nan Elliot
"I'd Swap My Old Skidoo For You"

Tlingit woman models decorative attire VINCE STREANO

Practitioner of Tlingit woodcarving at work in the Indian Art Center in Haines RON SANFORD

Carving a raven canoe at Bartlett Cove, Glacier Bay
National Park RON SANFORD

*❝ 'I belong here. I can feel my ancestors
paddling their cedar canoes up Lynn canal.
It's a wonderful feeling to know that you
and your people have been here for
thousands and thousands of years.' ❞*

Rosita Worl
as quoted in *"I'd Swap My Old Skidoo For You"*

A fireworks display of lodgepole pine boughs in the West Chichagof Yakobi Wilderness CARR CLIFTON

42

Vines and rusted rings decorate a wall at Crow Creek Mine south of Anchorage CAROL HAVENS

43

Autumn tundra on Kesugi Ridge in Denali State Park, with Mt. McKinley posing above the clouds SCOTT T. SMITH

They were traveling steadily along, a great mass of dark-brown figures. . . . The total effect of sound, movement, the sight of those thousands of animals, the clear golden western sky, the last sunlight on the mountain slope, gave one a feeling of being a privileged onlooker at a rare performance—a performance in Nature's own way, in the setting of countless ages, ages before man. How fortunate we were. . .

Margaret E. Murie
Two In The Far North

Antlers away: the blur of caribou bulls on the run through fall-colored tundra in Denali National Park SCOTT PRICE

One of the historic buildings at Crow Creek Mine bedecked with antique implements and fresh flowers JANE GNASS

66 *Every one of the gold-rush towns had to be unusual. All the factors which combined to produce them were unusual. First, the presence of gold in the earth—call that providential or geologic as you will. Second, the character, the climate, the topography, of the land itself; a land more difficult to conquer could hardly be imagined. Third, the people—the many kinds of people who would be attracted to the promise and the challenge of the gold and the land.* 99

Margaret E. Murie
from *"Winter in Fairbanks"* in
The Reader's Companion to Alaska

Once part of the largest copper-producing operation in the world, the crimson buildings of Kennicott Mine near McCarthy now house ghosts and tourists TOM AND PAT LEESON

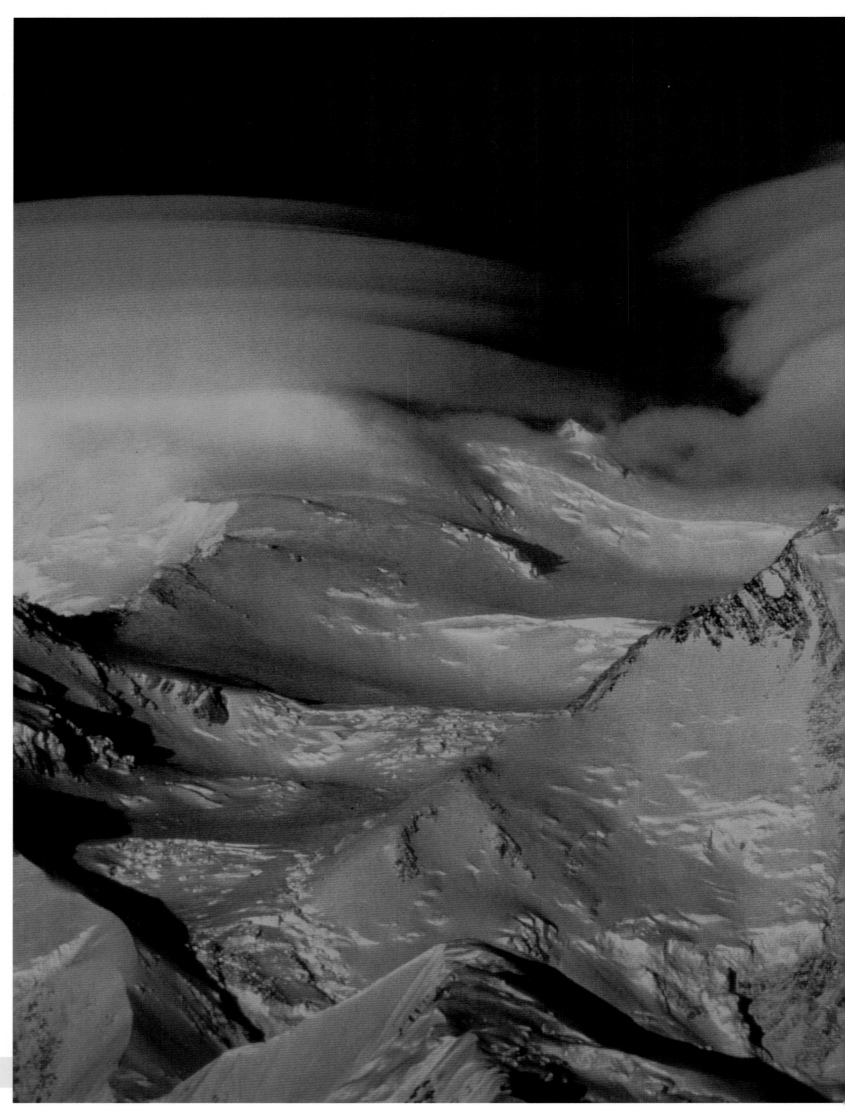

Lenticular clouds and early morning alpenglow embrace the summit contours of 20,320-foot Mt. McKinley RON SANFORD

We were startled by the sudden appearance of a red light burning with a strange unearthly splendor on the topmost peak. . . .Instead of vanishing as suddenly as it had appeared, it spread and spread until the whole range. . .was filled with the celestial fire. . . .we stood hushed and awe-stricken, gazing at the holy vision; and had we seen the heavens opened and God made manifest, our attention could not have been more tremendously strained.

John Muir, 1879
quoted in *The Reader's Companion to Alaska*

A primeval picture: a brown bear rises from the surface of Naknek Lake in Katmai National Park KENNAN WARD

Impressive brown bear tracks traverse the sand near the Copper River RICH REID

Mother brown bear and her cub survey part of the McNeil River State Game Sanctuary ROBIN BRANDT

"No sight encountered in the wilds. . . is quite so impressive as that of the great bear stalking across some mountain slope with the fur of his silvery robe rippling over his mighty muscles. His is a dignity and power matched by no other in the North American wilderness. To share a mountain with him for a while is a privilege and an adventure like no other."

Andy Russell
Grizzly Country

The historic buildings of Fort Seward catch the light beneath the Chilkat Range in Haines JOHN HYDE

" *Alaska is a melting pot. . . .There are those whose families have been here for centuries and those who recently pulled up roots to come. They came from the north and the south, from across the ocean and over the pole, from small farms and the world's largest cities.*

One thing Alaskans have in common: they either love this place or they hate it—sometimes in the same week. There is nothing lukewarm about living here. "

Nan Elliot
"I'd Swap My Old Skidoo For You"

Juneau, the state capital of Alaska, nestled between Gastineau Channel and Mount Juneau JEFF GNASS

A barnacled humpback whale breaches the waters of the Inside Passage JOHN HYDE

A sea otter grooms its fur HENRY H. HOLDSWORTH

" The great sea
Has set me adrift
It moves me like the weed in
a great river
Earth and the great weather
Move me,
Have carried me away
And move my inward parts
with joy. "

Osarqaq

A view of Valdez Arm and the abrupt coastline rise of the Chugach Mountains JAMES RANDKLEV

More than half of the 800 miles of the Trans-Alaska Pipeline rides on supports in a zig-zag pattern to flex with changes in the unstable permafrost beneath TOM AND PAT LEESON

State colors, blue and gold, on the Alaska Railroad as it crosses Twenty-Mile River near Portage JANE GNASS

Evening twilight beautifies a pulp mill and log pond
at Ward Cove near Ketchikan JEFF GNASS

*" The frontier spirit may be a romantic
notion. Then again, it may be a hard-nose,
driving necessity to go out and challenge
oneself, the world, whatever. Challenge,
excitement, adventure. . . it's ancient. "*

Nan Elliot
I'd Swap My Old Skidoo For You

59

Clearing fog reveals a calm day in Frederick Sound, Tongass National Forest CARR CLIFTON

Golden-crowned sparrow in full song
on Round Island HENRY H. HOLDSWORTH

" *We stood there for a long time, just looking. This might be our farthest north, ever. . . .In a tiny birch tree, a white-crowned sparrow, the voice of the arctic summer—'You will remember; you will remember,' he sang.* "

Margaret E. Murie
Two in the Far North

Brands of Alaskan fireweed complete with Mt. McKinley for prominence in this view in Denali National Park CARR CLIFTON

> *...and ever and anon amid all this wild auroral splendor some huge new-born berg dashes the living water into yet brighter foam, and the streaming torrents pouring from its sides are worn as robes of light, while they roar in awful accord with the winds and waves, deep calling unto deep, glacier to glacier, from fiord to fiord...*

John Muir
Travels in Alaska

A kayaker glides past glacial ice   JEFF FOOTT

Ice calving off the tidewater face of Hubbard Glacier into Disenchantment Bay,
Wrangell-St. Elias National Park and Preserve   TOM BEAN

The fabulously sculpted interior of an ice cave in Muir Glacier, Glacier National Park and Preserve   TOM BEAN

❝In civilization there is a vast, overwhelming whimper to be secure, sheltered, cared for. But if you refuse danger too much, you refuse life. . . .Either you must cover every chance, or trust yourself and go free, not tethered like Gulliver among the Lilliputians by a thousand threads of caution.❞

Lois Crisler
Arctic Wild

Gulls ride an iceberg in Tracy Arm   JOHN HYDE

A study in micro-pathfinding as climbers ascend Ruth Glacier in Denali National Park KENNAN WARD

Ice-fishing for land-locked silver salmon is a family affair in Matanuska Valley   LON E. LAUBER

" *'Part of the reason I stay is that I love the winter. The nice thing about winter is that it chases out a lot of people.'* "

Jim Babb
as quoted in *"I'd Swap My Old Skidoo For You"*

Playing in a snow cave   ROLLIE OSTERMICK

A skier drops a cliff at 15,000 feet on Mt. McKinley GLENN RANDALL

Anchorage in dusky winter light burns between the somnolent slopes of the Chugach Mountains
and the glassy peace of Cook Inlet ALLEN PRIER/ALASKA STOCK IMAGES

❝ *In Anchorage, the mountains seemed to fill the sky. There were the sharp ice and rock lines of the peaks in the Chugach Range to the east, the Chigmits in the west, and the Talkeetnas and the Alaska Range to the north. Thousands of unclimbed and even unnamed mountains rose straight from fjords of the Pacific, from spruce and birch forests of the interior, and from the treeless expanse of the Arctic tundra. Everywhere the land seemed to be bursting with incredible wildness.* ❞

Art Davidson
Minus 148º: The Winter Ascent of Mt. McKinley

The Russian Orthodox Church is a symbol of the past and present in the Russian Community in Ninilchik JEFF GNASS

❝ *Alaskans are like their Russian predecessors in that they have a great passion for the country. It is . . . that passion, which drove them to work for statehood long, hard, and consistently. . . .* **❞**

Hector Chevigny
Russian America

Reverent works gleam within St. Michael's Cathedral in Sitka VINCE STEANO

Colorful flowers set off the porcelain appearance of the Governor's Mansion in Juneau JEFF GNASS

Restricted travel in Denali National Park helps to preserve wildlife, habitat, and this view of Mt. McKinley from Stoney Hill Overlook CRAIG BRANDT

❝ Sunshine streamed through the luminous fringes of the clouds and fell on the green waters of the fiord, the glittering bergs, the crystal bluffs of the vast glacier, the intensely white, far-spreading fields of ice, and the ineffably chaste and spiritual heights . . .The whole making a picture of icy wilderness unspeakably pure and sublime.❞

John Muir
"First Sight of Glacier Bay, 1879"
in *The Reader's Companion to Alaska*

The glamorous reflections of cruise ship M/V Dalphne on the waters of Juneau's Gastineau Channel JEFF GNASS

Small icebergs from Margerie Glacier speckle the path of a cruise ship through Tarr Inlet in Glacier Bay National Park JEFF GNASS

Backpackers awaken to a glorious morning in Glacier Bay National Park JEFF GNASS

As seen from the lush summertime skirt of Adak Island, Great Sitkin Island rises 5,700 feet above the waters of the Bering Sea LON E. LAUBER

An intimate moment for a pair of horned puffins HENRY H. HOLDSWORTH

The mountains of Baranof Island lord over fishing vessels in Sitka Harbor CARR CLIFTON

66 *In the slow swell of dawn, the sea stretched before us like time, large enough to swallow all history, legend, desire, imagination. . . .We sailed on an ocean awash in the stories of all those who came before us in cedar canoes, sloops of war, merchant schooners, steamers, freighters, fishing boats, dories. In the ghostly light, they moved with us—the Tlingit Indians; the Russian, British, and American explorers; the seafarers and traders; the settlers and sailors; everyone who ever imagined themselves, like me, to be the first to witness this place.* **99**

Sherry Simpson
"Circumnavigation" in *Alaska Passages*

79

A long-billed dowitcher maintains a
watchful eye while feeding JOHN HYDE

A tundra pond reflects a peaceful late summer sky in Alaska's interior CARR CLIFTON

A style never to be duplicated decorates the Arctic Brotherhood Hall in Skagway's Historic District   JEFF GNASS

Gold! We leapt from our benches. Gold!
We sprang from our stools.
    Gold! We wheeled in the furrow, fired
with the faith of fools.
    Fearless, unfound, unfitted, far from the
night and the cold,
    Heard we the clarion summons,
followed the master-lure—Gold!

Robert Service
"The Trail of Ninety-eight"

A reminder of gold strikes and boom-or-bust days
of Skagway   CAROL HAVENS

Ready to fill your tank with horsepower, these old red pumps in Gustavus look like uniformed attendants TOM TILL

Spirit houses of the Eklutna Indians rest neatly in cemetery rows RON SANFORD

Fishing in Alaska is as much an opportunity for panorama as it is a sporting pursuit BARRY AND CATHY BECK

93

A young angler proudly presents his catch
ALISSA CRANDALL

A wolf deciding on a sockeye salmon dinner in Katmai National Park ROLLIE OSTERMICK

An angler admires the iridescent beauty of an arctic grayling LINDA CAUBLE

Anchored drift boats wait for the salmon to hit on the Kasilof River on the Kenai Peninsula LON E. LAUBER

King salmon are a prize at any size and this one looks to be a keeper BARRY AND CATHY BECK

66 *The king salmon has a special place in the heart of the Alaska angler.*

Mostly the optimistic fishermen wait—and hope. They dream of catching king salmon the size of an elementary-school child, of hooking a single fish that will fill the freezer with a week's worth of dinners.

They call them kings for short, but they don't call them kings for nothing. 99

Lew Freedman
Wild Times in *Wild Places*

At Punchbowl Lake the only sounds are water falling, the dip of oars, and the click of a camera shutter TOM BEAN

" Some of the near-by mountain cliffs rose 15,000 feet straight up from the sea. I said to myself: 'This is what you have been waiting for all your life. This is adventure. This is it.'. . . We knew now . . .that Alaska would exact her toll for what she gave. She would retain us for a little while on this detour—yes, longer than we had expected. To see the sights we wanted to see in the way we wanted to see them meant still further waiting and working and becoming Alaskans."

Constance Helmericks
"Newlyweds Head North" in
The Reader's Companion to Alaska

A float plane also makes a handy fishing boat in the Duncan Salt Chuck Wilderness JOHN HYDE

Paddling straight to adventure on Northwestern Lagoon in Kenai Fjords National Park TOM BEAN

A coastal peak shrouded in clouds in Kenai Fjords National Park on the Kenai Peninsula RICH REID

* This is different, unique, tough country. . . A guy has to know what he's doing. Flying is a way of life up here, and you have to get used to it. You can't drive. You can't walk. You can't swim.*

a Sitka pilot quoted in
Coming Into the Country,
by John McPhee

Small planes are the staple of supply transport to Alaskan villages LON E. LAUBER

A bush plane circles "The Maidens," part of the granite spires of Arrigetech Peaks in Gates of the Arctic National Park and Preserve JEFF GNASS

Perfectly adapted to their environment, this polar bear mother and her cubs will search year-round for food TOM AND PAT LEESON

Muskox bulls on Nunivak Island form a defensive ring LON E. LAUBER

An Inupiat girl poses in Barrow, the northern most community in the United States at approximately 71 degrees latitude north RANDY BRANDON/ ALASKA STOCK IMAGES

A house in Valdez is buried by a late spring snowfall ALISSA CRANDALL

66 The people of Alaska made their own exuberant way of life. Cold and dark could not defeat them. It was not easy to get into that country—it was not easy to get out of it. 99

Margaret E. Murie
Untamed Alaska

A winter day in Fairbanks: –44 degrees, 4 hours of daylight, and ice fog CRAIG BRANDT

Coldfoot can be reached by auto on the James Dalton Highway between
Fairbanks and Prudhoe Bay GEORGE WUERTHNER

A couple watches the sunset over Turnagain Arm, just south of Anchorage on the Seward Highway CLIFF RIEDINGER

Uniquely patterned stones in Wrangell-St. Elias National Park and Preserve ART WOLFE

Sunrise to sunset in one hour on the winter solstice in the Alaska Range CRAIG BRANDT

Coral and marine fossils that might be mistaken for petroglyphs found along the Canning River on the North Slope ART WOLFE

Children gaze up the trunks of old growth along Rainbow Falls Trail in the Tongass National Forest near Wrangell JOHN HYDE

'Oh! Don't you have flowers in Atka?' she asked.
'Yes, we have many,' he answered.
'Well, then, who plants them and takes
care of them?'
'God does," he told her. "We must enjoy them.'

Journal of an Aleutian Year

Alert hoary marmot offsets the brilliant
magenta of fireweed KENNAN WARD

Dwarf fireweed and yellow and red paintbrush pop with color along the banks of the Alsek River
and the Brabazon Range in Glacier Bay National Park CARR CLIFTON

Pond lilies and mare's tail are alive and thriving in Deadman Lake, Tetlin National Wildlife Refuge HARRY M. WALKER

Near extinction in the 1930s, trumpeter swans now number in the thousands in Alaska ART WOLFE

A waterfall forces a bright opening in a thicket of willows and alders near Juneau JEFF GNASS

Paintbrush find the ingredients to bloom in the granular soil near the St. Elias mountains
of Glacier Bay National Park CARR CLIFTON

A common redpoll grips his perch on a caribou antler HENRY H. HOLDSWORTH

The blanket toss is traditional, cultural and just plain fun for locals and visitors in Kotzebue

Aurora borealis dance in the sky over Denali National Park RON SANFORD

" I turned to go. Just then, my eyes caught sight of the northern lights above the black mountain at the far end of the lake. Curtains and ribbons of eerie green light swayed and twisted silently as charged particles riding the solar wind performed their cosmic waltz in the Earth's upper atmosphere. I stood for awhile, spellbound, watching the mysterious aurora borealis and listening to the two brown bears rumble across the stream. And I thought to myself, this is quintessential Alaska. "

Leon Kolankiewicz
Where Salmon Come to Die

Fiery wonder and frigid reality ignite the senses on a winter night in the Yanert Valley
just east of Denali National Park CRAIG BRANDT

Visitors skirt the gorge cut by the Lethe River in the Valley of Ten Thousand Smokes, Katmai National Park ROLLIE OSTERMICK

" The whole valley, as far as they could see, was filled with hundreds, thousands, tens of thousands of smokes, some large, some small . . . . the place boiled and eddied with clouds of vapor as if all the steam engines in the world had popped their safety valves at once. "

Rex Beach
Personal Exposures

Aerial view of the crater of Novarupta in the Valley of Ten Thousand Smokes ROLLIE OSTERMICK

The Mt. Katmai caldera is a splash of vibrant aqua in an otherwise bleak, volcanic landscape ROLLIE OSTERMICK

*" It was a breath-taking sight and quite unlike anything on the face of this globe.
A burnt and scalded mountain valley, pockmarked with pitholes which spouted
steam and smoke; a lonesome, snow-encircled place that boiled and simmered
amid Arctic desolation. "*

Rex Beach
Personal Exposures

Ice from Columbia Glacier litters the waters in front of Growler Bay RICH REID

66 I wanted the gold, and I got it—
Came out with a fortune last fall,—
Yet somehow life's not what I thought it,
And somehow the gold isn't all.

No! There's the land. (Have you seen it?)
It's the cussedest land that I know. . . .
Some say God was tired when He made it;
Some say it's a fine land to shun;
Maybe; but there's some as would trade it
For no land on earth—and I'm one. 99

Robert Service
"The Spell of the Yukon"

117

Only two were willing to venture onto the layered ice of a glacial pond on Root Glacier
in the Wrangell-St. Elias National Park and Preserve RICH REID

they made it possible

Alaska on My Mind would have been impossible to produce without the keen eyes and technical skills of more than thirty-five professional photographers. These women and men submitted their finest images, and the results show in this stunning collection of photos. What does not show is the work it took to get these images— the early mornings to capture the sunrise, the long climbs through rugged terrain, the endless hours of waiting for the perfect light, the hundreds of shots that didn't turn out quite right, and the high level of technical skill that was acquired through years of experience and study. To all the photographers who contributed to *Alaska on My Mind,* we say thanks. We appreciate their art and their hard work.

Michael S. Sample and Bill Schneider
Publishers, Falcon

Photographers in *Alaska on My Mind*

R.E. Barber
Tom Bean
Barry and Cathy Beck
Craig Brandt
Robin Brandt
Carr Clifton
Alissa Crandall
Jeff Foott
Lee Foster
Jane Gnass/
 Jon Gnass Photo Images
Jeff Gnass
Carol Havens
Henry H. Holdsworth
John Hyde
Donald M. Jones
Gary Lackie
Lon E. Lauber
Tom and Pat Leeson
Rollie Ostermick
Scott Price
Glen Randall
James Randklev
Rich Reid
Cliff Riedinger
Ron Sanford
Scott T. Smith
Vince Streano
Tom Till
Larry Ulrich
Harry Walker
Kennan Ward
Art Wolfe
George Wuerthner

Alaska Stock Images
 Chris Arend
 Randy Brandon
 Clark James Mishler
 Allen Prier

© 1998 by Falcon® Publishing Inc.
Helena, Montana

All rights reserved, including the right to reproduce any part of this book in any form, except brief quotations for reviews, without the written permission of the publisher.

Design, typesetting, and other prepress work by Falcon®, Helena, Montana.
Printed in Hong Kong

Library of Congress Number: 98-092650

ISBN 1-56044-382-0

For extra copies of this book please check with your local bookstore, or write Falcon® P.O. Box 1718, Helena, MT 59624 or call toll-free 1-800-582-2665.

End papers: bull moose in Wonder Lake, Denali National Park ROLLIE OSTERMICK

acknowledgments

The publisher gratefully acknowledges the following sources:

Title page and pages 34, 40, 41, 54, 59, 66, and 90 quotes from *"I'd Swap My Old Skidoo for You,"* by Nan Elliot. Sammamish Press, Issaquah, Wash., 1989.

Page 3 quote from *Wilderness,* by Rockwell Kent. Wesleyan University Press, Hanover, N.H., 1996.

Pages 7 and 120 quotes from *Alaska: The Great Country,* by Ella Higginson. Macmillan Co., New York, 1908.

Page 9 quote from *My Wilderness: The Pacific West,* by William O. Douglas. Doubleday & Co., New York, 1960.

Page 11 quote from *The Stars, the Snow, the Fire,* by John Haines. Washington Square Press, New York, 1989.

Pages 15, 44, and 60 quotes from *Two In the Far North,* by Margaret E. Murie. Alfred A. Knopf, New York, 1962.

Page 16 quote from "Address to the American Meteorological Society," by Ernest Gruening, in *An Alaskan Reader,* ed. by Ernest Gruening. Meredith Press, New York, 1966.

Page 18 quote from *Ten Thousand Miles With a Dog Sled,* by Hudson Stuck. Charles Scribner's Sons, New York, 1916.

Page 24 quote from *Fishcamp,* by Nancy Lord. Island Press, Washington, D.C., 1997.

Page 27 quote from "When the Water Died," by Walter Meganack, Sr., in *Season of Dead Water,* ed. by Helen Frost. Breitenbush Books, Portland, Ore., 1990.

Pages 30 and 64 quotes from *Arctic Wild,* by Lois Crisler. Harper & Row, New York, 1958.

Page 33 quote from *An Alaskan Reader,* ed. by Ernest Gruening. Meredith Press, New York, 1966.

Page 39 quote from *Henry Thoreau and John Muir Among the Indians,* by Richard F. Fleck. Archon Books, Hamden, Conn., 1985.

Page 46 quote from "Winter in Fairbanks," by Margaret E. Murie, in *The Reader's Companion to Alaska,* ed. by Alan Ryan. Harcourt Brace & Co., San Diego and New York, 1997.

Page 48 quote from *Mountain Wilderness,* by William R. Hunt. Alaska Natural History Association, Anchorage, 1996.

Page 51 quote from *The Reader's Companion to Alaska,* ed. by Alan Ryan. Harcourt Brace & Co., San Diego and New York, 1997.

Page 52 quote from *The Grizzlies of Mount McKinley,* by Adolph Murie. University of Washington Press, Seattle, 1987. Originally published by National Park Service, 1981.

Pages 53 and 86 quotes from *Grizzly Country,* by Andy Russell. Alfred A. Knopf, New York, 1967.

Page 56 quote from *Earth and the Great Weather,* by Kenneth Brower. Friends of the Earth, New York, n.d.

Page 62 quote from *Travels in Alaska,* by John Muir. Houghton Mifflin Co., Boston, 1979.

Page 69 quote from *Minus 148° : The Winter Ascent of Mt. McKinley,* by Art Davidson. W.W. Norton & Co., New York, 1969.

Page 70 quote from *Russian America,* by Hector Chevigny. Viking Press, New York, 1965.

Page 72 quote from *One Alaskan's Potpourri,* by H.P. "Pappy" Moss. Eagle River Type and Graphics, Eagle River, Alaska, 1997.

Page 74 quote from "First Sight of Glacier Bay, 1879," by John Muir, in *The Reader's Companion to Alaska,* ed. by Alan Ryan. Harcourt Brace & Co., San Diego and New York, 1997.

Page 79 quote from "Circumnavigation," by Sherry Simpson, in *Alaska Passages,* ed. by Susan Fox Rogers. Sasquatch Books, Seattle, 1996.

Pages 80 and 98 quotes from *Coming Into the Country,* by John McPhee. Farrar, Straus & Giroux, New York, 1977.

Page 82 quote from "The Trail of Ninety-eight," by Robert Service, in *Collected Poems of Robert Service.* Dodd, Mead & Co., New York, 1940.

Page 84 quote from *Whales, Ice, and Men,* by John R. Bockstoce. University of Washington Press, Seattle, 1986.

Page 93 quote from *Anchorage Altogether,* by Corrie Player and Sheryl White, 1972.

Page 95 quote from *Wild Times in Wild Places,* by Lew Freedman. Glacier Press, Anchorage, 1996.

Page 96 quote from "Newlyweds Head North," by Constance Helmericks, in *The Reader's Companion to Alaska,* ed. by Alan Ryan. Harcourt Brace & Co., San Diego and New York, 1997.

Page 102 quote from introduction to *Untamed Alaska,* ed. by Elizabeth L.T. Brown and Carolyn M. Clark. Thomasson-Grant, Charlottesville, Va., 1987.

Page 106 quote from *Journal of an Aleutian Year,* by Ethel Ross Oliver. University of Washington Press, Seattle, 1988.

Page 112 quote from *Where Salmon Come to Die,* by Leon Kolankiewicz. Pruett Publishing, Boulder, Colo., 1993.

Pages 114 and 115 quotes from *Personal Exposures,* by Rex Beach. Harper & Row, New York, 1940.

Page 116 quote from "The Spell of the Yukon," by Robert Service, in *Collected Poems of Robert Service.* Dodd, Mead & Co., New York, 1940.

A bald eagle soars in a blazing Alaskan sunset TOM AND PAT LEESON

66 *'I don't know what it is that keeps pulling me back to this country,' said a man one day. . . . 'Maybe you see a white mountain, or a green valley, or a big river, or a blue strait, or a waterfall—and like a flash your heart opens, and shuts in an ache for Alaska that stays! . . . No, I don't know* what *it is, but I do know* how *it is; and so does every other poor devil that ever heard that something calling him that's just Alaska. . . .I tell you what, if ever a country had a spirit, it's Alaska; and when it once gets hold of you and gets to calling you to come, you might just as well get up and start, for it calls you and follows you, and haunts you till you do.'* 99

Ella Higginson
Alaska: The Great Country